Bunny Buddhism

Bunny Buddhism

Hopping Along the Path to Enlightenment

Krista Lester

A PERIGEE BOOK

A PERIGEE BOOK
Published by the Penguin Group
Penguin Group (USA) LLC
375 Hudson Street, New York, New York 10014

USA · Canada · UK · Ireland · Australia · New Zealand · India · South Africa · China

penguin.com

A Penguin Random House Company

Library of Congress Cataloging-in-Publication Data

Lester, Krista.
Bunny Buddhism : hopping along the path to enlightenment / Krista Lester.
pages cm
ISBN 978-0-399-16787-4 (pbk.)
1. Rabbits—Humor. 2. Zen Buddhism—Humor.
3. Spiritual life—Zen Buddhism. I. Title.
PN6231.R23L46   2014
818'.602—dc23   2013039972

First edition: April 2014

PRINTED IN THE UNITED STATES OF AMERICA

10 9 8 7 6 5 4 3 2 1

Text design by Tiffany Estreicher

For my parents

Introduction

A few years ago, I found myself facing the familiar feeling that life was pointless and I would always be miserable. The feeling arrived every so often and would consume my life for weeks, months, or even years at a time. I braced myself for the depression and anxiety, panic attacks, and inexplicable physical pain. But this time, something was a little bit different. I was fed up. I was tired of being pushed around by my own thoughts. I was determined—*absolutely determined*—to take control and to stop the cycle of misery from playing out for the rest of my life.

When I couldn't come up with any better ideas, I decided to sit down and make a list of things that make me smile. I have always believed practice makes perfect, so I thought maybe I could learn to be happy if I just practiced smiling. It sounded kind of ridiculous, but I planned to try it until I either proved the theory wrong or came up with a better idea. I had to think hard—*really hard*—to come up with anything at all to put on the list. And then I remembered my late Mini Rex rescue bunny, Lloyd. I cried and smiled all at once with the memory, and bunnies went on the list.

For the second item, I was stuck and had to shift my approach. I tried to imagine who *does* smile and was shocked when the image of a smiling Buddha appeared in my head. It was confusing. I knew absolutely nothing about Buddhism, but I was intrigued. So I bought some books, began to meditate, and eventually added Buddhism to the list. Some of the first books I read convinced me that meditation and repeated use of certain pathways in the brain can actually change the structure of the brain, so I was beginning to believe I really *could* make a habit of smiling simply by practicing. I vowed to think of both items on my list at least once a day for the foreseeable future. To hold myself accountable and to keep a tally of accumulated smiles, I decided to post my Bunny Buddhism thoughts on Twitter.

At first, I was inspired by some great Buddhist writers, most notably His Holiness the Dalai Lama, Thich Nhat Hanh, Pema Chödrön, Yongey Mingyur Rinpoche, and Ezra Bayda. Before long, I was reading primary Buddhist texts. For instruction in meditation, I listened to Jon Kabat-Zinn and began to attend meditation sits with Profound Existence, the Boston chapter of Noah Levine's Dharma Punx—an inspiring group of people I could relate to. Beyond these, I took inspiration from Taoism and Christianity, as well as some historical figures, whenever I felt the principles overlapped with Buddhist ones. Finally, more and more inspiration came to me from people who started to read, retweet, and comment on my Twitter feed. I owe a debt of gratitude to each of these people, and many others, who have played a vital role in restoring my faith in humanity and helping me remember how to smile.

Now, it is several years later, and Bunny Buddhism has become an important part of my daily routine. As it turns out, the little bit of positivity I put out there in the world has, much to my surprise, resulted in more positivity. The experience has helped me reframe my entire outlook on the world. While I have learned a lot, I know I can't claim to be a great Buddhist. But I do try my best to stay true to the spirit of peace and compassion that I understand to be at the heart of Buddhism. And my intention with Bunny Buddhism is what it has always been: to bring a smile with the hope that one smile might lead to another and another.

Bunny Wisdom

Know well what leads you forward and
what holds you back, and choose the path
that leads to bunniness.

✧

A bunny who is happy and peaceful
brings joy wherever he hops.

✧

The wise bunny knows we rarely see
things as they are; we see them as we
believe them to be.

We must choose our hops
carefully for others will see them
and be influenced by them.

※

When bunniness seems far away,
one must pause and breathe deeply
to find it again.

※

A potato is a potato no matter
how much I want it to be a carrot.

The wise bunny knows there are always
more fields of clover to discover.

⁂

Bunniness never decreases
by being shared.

⁂

Even a reliable bunny misses
a hop sometimes; then the
important thing becomes simply to
return to hopping.

Winning gives birth to hostility.
Losing, one lies down in pain. The wise
bunny is calm, having set winning
and losing aside.

When the bunny is ready,
bunniness will appear.

The bunny who is awake will no longer
be afraid of nightmares.

Joy comes from helping other bunnies.
Suffering comes from wanting bunniness
only for oneself.

˅

May we all find the alert stillness
of our bunny natures.

˅

The wise bunny knows that freedom
comes from tearing down barriers rather
than building them up.

Simple things can be extraordinary to
the bunny who chooses to see them.

The fear of failure can
prevent a bunny from seeing how
far he can really hop.

✻

Bunniness comes from within.
Do not seek it without.

✻

The compassionate bunny
cares for all creatures,
without exception.

The wise bunny does not look back in anger or forward in fear, but around in awareness.

There is a path, and I can hop it.

The smallest amount of bunniness dedicated to others is more precious than anything dedicated to oneself.

When a bunny believes in herself, there
is no need to convince others.

彩

A kind bunny is always willing to
lend a helping hop.

彩

To act from bunniness for the sake of
all is the greatest gift I can give.

The wise bunny knows it is better to sit,
hop, or bound than to wobble.

In trying to be like another bunny,
I fail to learn how to be myself.

The bunny who chews at his
wound does not allow it to heal.

When there are carrots, one must
not eat them all at once.

Even the bunny who has found
bunniness must continue to practice it.

The wise bunny never delays the expression of sincere gratitude.

✟

As bunniness grows within me, hatred falls away.

✟

There are hops that are dark with dark result and hops that are bright with bright result.

Each day that I wake up is a brand-new day to share bunniness with others.

The bunny who makes a mistake and doesn't correct it is making another mistake.

I am but the continuation of the bunnies who came before me.

Hopping without expectation does not mean hopping without purpose.

We must consider the pawprints we leave on this Earth so future bunnies will have a place to hop.

One cannot find bunniness if one is not willing to face what lies within.

The wise bunny knows the carrot
will not hop to him.

Sorrow is knowledge; bunnies who know
the most have mourned the deepest.

❧

Bunniness requires patience with oneself.

❧

A bunny hopping the path he
was born to hop does not wonder how
he compares to others.

No bunny exists entirely alone;
everything is in relation to everything else.

One who chooses to live in bunniness
must choose it anew day after day.

A foolish bunny is happy until his
mischief catches up with him.

One must only hop when the hop will
be both friendly and sincere.

Bunniness lives in the midst of destruction,
never to be destroyed.

A bunny describing another bunny
often reveals more of himself than
of the other bunny.

The wise bunny recognizes an end as
the beginning of something new.

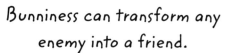

Bunniness can transform any
enemy into a friend.

A bunny does not find peace until he
extends the circle of his compassion to
include all bunnies.

✯

The path appears for the bunny
who forges ahead.

✯

Without knowledge, there is no bunniness.
Without bunniness, there is no knowledge.

There have to be evil bunnies so good
bunnies will know how not to hop.

The only truly rich bunny is the one who
realizes he has enough carrots.

There is no need to prove to others
how much bunniness one has.

To work toward peace for all,
a bunny must have peace within.

✓

Breathing in, I know I am a bunny.
Breathing out, I know pretending to be
a wolf will not serve me well.

✓

To be constant in bunniness,
one must be willing to change.

Hops that do not come from love
are likely to come from fear.

✲

The wise bunny knows this moment
waits as if one has never wasted
a moment before.

✲

Bunniness is the liberation of the bunny
we are no longer afraid to become.

A happy bunny doesn't mind the rain;
therefore, let it rain.

No bunny can love without
exposing his heart.

∀

At times, we all need an
expression of bunniness. Let us extend
bunniness to others, that we might
inspire them to do the same.

∀

Big hops and little hops are
equally important.

The wise bunny knows that courage comes from knowing something is more important than fear.

A generous bunny is never poor.

We all need carrots and bunniness: carrots to feed the stomach and bunniness to feed the heart.

The bunny who hops a path different
from mine is not necessarily lost.

May we all live in joy and bunniness,
even when we have nothing.

Much time is lost in waiting
for another bunny to express what
we already know.

A compassionate bunny does not turn
away from another bunny's pain.

Forgiveness is an attribute of
strong bunnies.

One need not know why
the nose twitches but simply know
that it twitches.

One must not hop so much that one
forgets to experience bunniness.

The wise bunny becomes wise by asking
what he does not know.

The doors of bunniness are never shut.

The law of cause and effect is
uniform and without exception;
all bunnies are what their past
hops have made them.

The bunny who tries not to suffer
only suffers more.

As with all things, one must be careful
not to take bunniness too seriously.

❦

Upon seeing his own faults, the wise
bunny abandons them.

❦

Hopping down another bunny's path
will rarely lead to bunniness.

The sweetness of a carrot
cannot be experienced by merely
hearing of its taste.

❦

Even my deepest fears do not compare
to my bunny courage.

❦

False bunniness is more dangerous
than a lack of bunniness.

The bunny who thinks
but does not hop
is like a flower that has
no fragrance.

The wise bunny knows
hopping too far is just as bad
as not hopping enough.

❧

Bunniness can never come at the
expense of another bunny.

❧

A successful bunny must never forget
the spirit of the beginner.

A believer in bunniness does not dispute
with any bunny in the world.

Ⅴ

If I fail, let it not be because
I was afraid to hop.

Ⅴ

The whole world changes
for a bunny who clearly sees the
beauty of a carrot.

For one who knows bunniness,
everything is as it needs to be.

✣

The bunny who thinks tomorrow
is the time will suddenly find that
life has slipped away.

✣

A bunny is not considered a good bunny
just because he is good at hopping.

The wise bunny knows the
presence of fear means only that fear
is present, and nothing more.

Bunniness can be found even in
bunnies we don't like very much.

Sometimes joy is the source of a hop,
and sometimes a hop is the source of joy.

The wise bunny observes without
trying to control.

Without bunniness, there is no clarity;
there is only a bunny's perception
of the world.

A bunny's greatest glory is not never
falling, but rising each time he falls.

❦

No other bunny can live
my life for me.

❦

Bunniness is found where it
already exists. Where it does not exist,
one must take it there.

The wise bunny does not worry if
no one knows of him; he just seeks
to be worth knowing.

☙

It is better to hop than to think of hopping.

☙

Hop for the good of the many,
for the bunniness of the many, and
out of compassion for the world.

Breathing in, at this moment,
I need not hop. Breathing out, I free
myself from the urge to hop.

A bunny can only lose what he clings to.

You can never offer bunniness
too soon, for you never know how
soon it will be too late.

We are all bunnies in the same
vast field of clover.

A bunny grounded in bunniness finds
no obstacles in his path.

Every hop is joy,
and every breath is peace.

The wise bunny knows to live
in the world that is rather than the
world that should be.

Success is not the key to bunniness;
bunniness is the key to success.

✦

If you can hop mindfully once,
you can do it again.

✦

The compassionate bunny never
eats a carrot without sharing
it in some way.

What lies behind us and what lies
before us are small matters compared
to the bunniness within us.

᭜

Wise bunnies make more opportunities
than they find.

᭜

Even the smallest and least significant hop
has an effect on the universe.

I do not need to say "I am a bunny"
to be a bunny.

Without inner bunniness,
outer bunniness is not possible.

A bunny blinded by belligerence
can never take good advice.

꙳

Small hop, small bunniness.
No hop, no bunniness.

꙳

Even the bunny who has
suffered because of love can
learn to love again.

The first hop is never perfect,
but it is a necessary starting point
for all hopping improvements.

The first hop is never perfect,

There can be no bunniness where
ignorance reigns.

I will not burden another bunny with
what I know to be unpleasant.

The wise bunny knows blame
does nothing to reduce suffering.

Bunniness is not learned in safety.
One must seek unfamiliar ground
and hop without fear.

A hop that is both true and kind
can change the world.

I will not allow fear of the
unknown to prevent me from
experiencing bunniness.

⋎

A bunny can neither be more
than a bunny nor less than a bunny.

⋎

Breathing in, I know that anger
is in me. Breathing out, I refrain
from hopping in anger.

A bunny life is but a flash of lightning
in a summer cloud.

The wise bunny welcomes adversity
as an unexpected gift.

⋎

Every hop has the potential
to be joyful.

⋎

The faults of other bunnies are
easy to perceive, but one's own faults
are difficult to perceive.

I will be my own bunny because
no two bunnies are the same, though
we all breathe the same air.

※

The best hop is not always the
first one to come to mind.

※

I suffer because all bunnies suffer,
and I take comfort in knowing
I am not alone.

A bunny hopping in circles will continue to hop in circles until she changes direction.

Ϋ

When eating a carrot, one must be there with the carrot.

Ϋ

The wise bunny knows compassion is not complete if it does not include oneself.

Every hop I have hopped is my future
as well as my past.

The wise bunny knows this storm will pass
and the sun will shine again.

The bunny who stays present in
discomfort even for a moment gradually
learns not to fear it.

✸

There is no place where bunniness is not.

✸

The more we try to hop away from pain,
the more it clings to us. One must learn to
find the bunniness within the pain.

May no bunny be unhappy, malicious,
ill, neglected, or despised.

❧

The challenge of bunniness is to hop
through life without losing oneself and
without imposing oneself on others.

❧

The wise bunny knows negativity
comes from resisting what is.

Today is the day to make
another bunny happy.

Y

Just as one lamp dispels ten thousand
years of darkness, one flash of
bunniness destroys ten thousand
years of ignorance.

Y

Being busy is no excuse for
hopping mindlessly.

My thoughts when I stumble
greatly influence the outcome
of my next hop.

❦

Wise bunnies and foolish bunnies
both have things to teach us.

❦

I know bunniness exists because
it is what arises when I sit calmly
with myself.

The wise bunny hops even when
the way is unclear.

Everything arises and passes away;
the bunny who sees this is above sorrow.

All a bunny has to do is be himself,
fully and authentically.

It is not enough to watch others hop;
one must hop one's own path with
steadfast aim.

The bunny who resists change misses the
opportunity to experience new joys.

❧

A bunny does not need to struggle
to be a bunny.

❧

Just one hop in the direction
of bunniness sets the wheel of
truth in motion.

It is better to hop slowly than to
stop hopping altogether.

✣

One must have devotion toward
those with bunniness and compassion
for those without.

✣

On a good day, I am a bunny.
On a bad day, I am still a bunny.

May bunniness be an island for
those who seek one and a lamp for
those desiring light.

The carrot may be eaten,
but it is never completely gone.

A compassionate bunny sees
himself in all others and all others
within himself.

☙

Life doesn't stop when I hop into a cave.

☙

Bunniness is everywhere,
but it is only seen by those who
have planted its seeds.

The wise bunny knows one
cannot control a result, only the
hop that leads to it.

☙

May wisdom and compassion
guide our hearts and our hops.

☙

Great compassion rises in
my heart for those without
knowledge of bunniness.

Disappointment is often just the beginning of a new path to hop.

There is no bunny in bunniness.

The wise bunny knows both gain and loss are impermanent, bound up with suffering, and subject to change.

May all bunnies hurt no one and
be consistent in well-doing.

✌

If any path is to be hopped,
let a bunny hop it vigorously.

✌

We must be willing to allow the
moment of bunniness to manifest
when all our defenses are down.

The dirt a bunny digs often
becomes the wall that separates
her from other bunnies.

If following the example of
another bunny, one must take care
not to abandon one's own truth.

҄

The wise bunny knows
spectacular hops are always preceded
by unspectacular preparation.

҄

It is when I see what bunniness is not
that I know what bunniness is.

Much suffering arises when a bunny
seeks happiness only for himself.

Ⓥ

As we hop, so we become.

Ⓥ

If there is not enough time for
every hop, one must determine which
hop will benefit the most bunnies,
and start there.

Breathing in, I know I am a bunny.
Breathing out, I know a bunny
is all I have to be.

☙

The wise bunny thinks lightly of
herself and deeply of the world.

☙

A generous heart, kind hops,
and a life of service and compassion are
the things that renew bunniness.

The field of clover becomes part of the
bunny who sits and contemplates it.

Bunniness does not eliminate pain,
it only makes it more bearable.

Bunniness is not the means to an end;
it is both the means and the end.

⅄

We must love other bunnies because
they are bunnies, not because they are
worthy or unworthy of our love.

⅄

No matter how far I hop, the path is
always there, before me and behind me.

Bunniness means recognizing others'
needs alongside one's own.

Ψ

May I fashion my life as a garland
of beautiful hops.

Ψ

The wise bunny knows much
time can be lost worrying about
wolves that never appear.

Let us hop carefully and do no harm,
for as we sow so shall we reap.

✧

To touch the true nature of bunniness,
one must also be willing to touch the
true nature of suffering.

✧

There is no such thing as a permanent me
because a bunny is always changing.

I cannot blame another bunny;
it is my own hops that have led me here.

✧

May the bunniness in this world
sustain me that I might find strength to
help relieve the suffering of others.

✧

Only the bunny who shares his carrots
has any real gain.

A bunny cannot withhold
bunniness, just as the sun cannot
withhold light.

The wise bunny knows a tree
does not use its leaves to hold on
to the wind.

One does not need to think of
bunniness while hopping because
hopping itself is bunniness.

To forgive the mistakes of other
bunnies is to be good to oneself.

One must hop directly into fear,
recognize it's there, and embrace
it with bunniness.

૪

There will always be foolish bunnies;
getting angry with them is like resenting
a fire for burning.

૪

Even a very careful bunny will
occasionally make an errant hop.

All beings possess the capacity
to be awakened to love, freedom,
and bunniness.

❧

I must be aware of my true bunny
nature so I will know if I've begun to hop
a path that's not quite right for me.

❧

The wise bunny knows pain is often a sign
of something that needs to change.

One must avoid evil hops as a bunny
who loves life avoids poison.

Having and losing are only
phases of bunniness.

We must help one another hop
through the muck and emerge in the
fields of clover.

꓿

The bunny who thinks someone
else is responsible is not taking responsibility
for her own bunniness.

꓿

Wherever there is a bunny, there
is the possibility of bunniness.

The wise bunny knows the rules well
so he can break them effectively.

⋎

This hop is the beginning
of all other hops.

⋎

One must be respectful of superiors,
considerate of inferiors, and sympathetic
for bunnies in trouble.

I would rather trust and be deceived
than distrust my fellow bunnies.

꙳

One must train for bunniness
one hop at a time.

꙳

It is the pressures, pains, and
risks of life that wake us up and lead
us to our vast bunny nature.

Happy bunnies are happy as a
result of their desire for the
happiness of others.

⅄

I cannot seek bunniness outside myself
because I myself am bunniness.

⅄

The wise bunny knows there is no
tomorrow, only a string of todays.

Hop as if you are carressing
the Earth with your paws.

Breathing in, I am aware of my bunny pain. Breathing out, I know my pain does not define me.

✙

I cannot impose self-discipline upon other bunnies.

✙

I know bunniness is real even if it cannot be perceived by the ordinary senses.

One must carefully manage
the bunny mind, for every hop
begins as a thought.

✔

The wise bunny knows that the sun
doesn't rush to rise or hesitate to set.

✔

It is difficult to maintain bunniness
while other bunnies are in pain.

May the bunny who does well
repeat his well-doing, and may the
bunny who is lost rediscover
his bunny nature.

Every hop counts.

There is no creature without bunniness,
just as there is no point of darkness
within the sun.

The grass will grow in spring whether
or not I am there to munch it.

The bunny who desires joy,
yet hurts others who also love joy,
will never obtain bunniness.

What I do for myself, I do for
other bunnies; what I do for other
bunnies, I do for myself.

🌱

The wise bunny knows that taking
no action means nothing will improve.

🌱

When I do good, and do it again
and again, bunniness is the outcome.

To know and not hop is not yet to know.

❧

One can always afford to share
the gifts of peace and bunniness.

❧

A half-eaten carrot is not a matter
of which half is gone and which remains;
it is simply a half-eaten carrot.

The wise bunny knows that the word "hop" is
not the same as an actual hop.

✑

I rejoice in bunniness and am
liberated from the non-bunniness inherent
to the cycle of existence.

✑

Woe to he who strikes a bunny; more woe
to the bunny who strikes back.

Better than a thousand aimless hops is a single hop in the way of peace.

※

In a sense, I am the same bunny I was yesterday, and, in a sense, I am different in every moment.

※

It is unwise to be too sure of one's own understanding of bunniness.

A carrot is even tastier when shared
with another bunny.

One must hop toward the light
rather than sit in a shadow and
wonder why it's dark.

✧

A bunny always has the option
to begin again.

✧

When the world is filled
with pain, one must transform the
pain into bunniness.

It is not hopping itself but
the awareness of hopping that
leads to bunniness.

Ψ

The bunny who allows the right
moment to pass suffers greatly.

Ψ

The wise bunny knows nothing grows
where no seeds are sown.

I do not hop because I know the way;
I hop because I have legs that can hop.

✴

When I am a sad bunny, I know
my sadness will return to bunniness just
as a wave returns to the sea.

✴

The kind bunny chooses gentleness and does
not want that which is taken by force.

No bunny can find bunniness for another;
we each must find our own.

The wise bunny accepts life for what it is,
not for what it is expected to be.

It would be a cause of regret for
bunniness to be shattered by an insatiable
desire for carrots.

֍

Sometimes choosing not to hop is
more powerful than hopping.

֍

The bunny who lights a lamp for
another also brightens his own path.

Bunniness is within me;
my only job is to help it shine through.

❧

Breathing in, I recognize my
bunny pain. Breathing out, I recognize
where I am not in pain.

❧

No bunny saves us but ourselves.
We ourselves must hop the path.

It can never hurt to think highly
of another bunny. Often their hops will
spread more joy because of it.

✼

In bunniness, there is no place for blame.

✼

One who has given up on bunnies
has given up on himself.

My neighbor's right to bunniness is
no greater and no lesser than my own.

⋎

To munch a carrot, one must be
willing to dig in the dirt.

⋎

The wise bunny sits like a
mountain, knowing no wind can blow
the mountain down.

One does not need to sit in a special
field of clover to find bunniness.

The bunny who opens up to love holds
the key to his own prison door.

❦

The bunny who wants to understand
truth must not become blinded by what
he wants to be true.

❦

May I counter each hurtful hop
I see with a hop in the name of love
and bunniness.

The wise bunny does not wait for
the right moment but makes this moment
the best it can be.

☙

Bunniness in us encourages
bunniness in others.

☙

The hop itself is more important
than the idea of a hop.

It is not the wolf but one's perception of
the wolf that causes fear.

⅄

A bunny can only learn what he has the
humility to admit he doesn't know.

⅄

The wise bunny frees her mind
from hate and pride, and gently hops
her way in peace.

Among bunnies not one is free
from blame; the bunny who sits is blamed
as well as the bunny who hops.

Bunniness begins when I begin to
accept my weaknesses.

One must remember that the
path exists even when the bunny mind
is too confused to see it.

There is never a wrong time for
a loving hop.

Compassionate bunniness is based
on fundamental rights and applies to
enemies as well as friends.

The wise bunny knows nothing is ever lost, and nothing is ever gained.

⋎

Living means choosing, and the way we choose to hop is infallibly and perfectly expressed in the hop itself.

⋎

All beings share the wish to avoid suffering and to know bunniness.

I am a bunny, and I will continue to be a bunny. I can either accept it or make myself miserable wishing it wasn't so.

When discouraged, the wise bunny encourages others.

Despair can only be defeated through bunniness and gratitude.

When a bunny finds light, it does not matter
how long he has been in darkness.

✿

Bunnies hop. It is neither good nor bad;
it simply is.

✿

One must produce bunniness where
it does not yet exist and increase bunniness
where it already exists.

The wise bunny knows to expect
all forms: sun bunny, moon bunny,
happy bunny, sad bunny.

Before enlightenment: chomp carrots, munch clover. After enlightenment: chomp carrots, munch clover.

꜀

Harm no bunny nor have them harmed.

꜀

May I embrace my bunny nature, and may it give me the courage to share bunniness with others.

When no bunny does the kind and helpful
thing, I will do it myself.

✧

A shadow may be invisible in the den,
but it always appears when one hops into
the sunshine.

✧

You cannot know bunniness if you
continue to deceive yourself.

There is a path to hop on, there is hopping
being done, but there is no hopper.

When I accept myself, I can
accept other bunnies, and only then
can I help change the world.

When all wish to injure has vanished,
pain will cease and bunniness will abound.

All bunnies suffer. Some suffer too much.
Some suffer too little.

I do not need to wait; the conditions for
bunniness are already here.

The wise bunny is ever vigilant and strives to avoid hopping into the cave of ignorance.

Tragedy often shows us the bunniness that connects us all.

May I take into my heart the suffering of all bunnies and return it to the world in the form of goodwill.

It is better for a bunny to hop alone than
to hop alongside a bunny who is selfish, vain,
quarrelsome, and obstinate.

The bunny mind is limited only by
ignorance.

Not to see bunniness is pain, and
it is pain to see what is not bunniness.

I hop because there are things that cannot be expressed by not hopping.

※

The wise bunny knows that the best way to take care of the future is to take care of the present.

※

One can go a long way toward bunniness by simply respecting the rights of others.

Bunnies whose minds are shaped by selfless
thoughts give joy wherever they hop.

Ⓥ

There are many paths but only
one bunniness.

Ⓥ

One bunny can influence another,
and another, and yet another until all
bunnies will benefit.

A bunny who hops across my path does not necessarily mean me any harm.

The wise bunny knows life is full of suffering
and chooses not to create more.

※

In moments when I cannot access my
inner bunniness, it is enough to know it is
still there somewhere.

※

If I hold a grudge against another bunny,
I am the one who suffers.

There are only two mistakes one can make along the path: not hopping all the way, and never beginning to hop.

☙

Bunniness is a light among those who hop in darkness.

☙

Bunnies call one carrot good and another carrot bad, but all that can really be said is that it's a carrot.

I cannot teach a bunny to swim if I myself
am carried away by the current.

� a small decorative mark

The bunny I am today comes from
the hops of yesterday.

The opportunity for bunniness is present
every time I meet another bunny.

All will become clear when one stops
following the ideas of others and begins
listening to one's inner voice of bunniness.

The carrot does not rot to spite me.

Present circumstances don't determine
where a bunny can go; they merely
determine where the journey begins.

॰⅄॰

The wise bunny knows there is no
cure for hot and cold.

॰⅄॰

A single day lived in bunniness
is better than a hundred years lived
without it.

May no bunny deceive and no bunny
wish for another to suffer.

※

Bunniness can only be found
when one has let go of all preconceived
notions of bunniness.

※

Memories of my bunny past cannot
hurt me in the here and now.

One must try not to judge
because no bunny is required to
meet another's expectations.

⋎

I do not know the hops that led
another bunny here.

⋎

My inner bunniness cannot be damaged
by uncertainty or change.

One must not be harsh with
any bunny; those who are treated harshly
will reply in the same way.

⁓

Bunniness inspires us. Non-bunniness
teaches us.

⁓

It is when it is most difficult to
love other bunnies that we must open
our hearts the most.

To appreciate the beauty of a
snowflake, a bunny must be willing
to sit in the cold.

All bunnies have bunniness, but only some choose to offer it openly.

Y

The wise bunny knows that if grief or anger arises, one must let there be grief or anger.

Y

Each hop is a journey and the journey itself is bunniness.

Other bunnies are probably not trying to
make me suffer. I choose to react
compassionately because they also suffer.

All bunnies everywhere deserve
to be loved.

Once knowing bunniness, losing it is
the only real tragedy in life.

A bunny who knows how hard it is to hop
does not judge other bunnies for hopping.

☖

The wise bunny knows a sunset does not
extinguish the sun.

☖

The more I am motivated by
bunniness, the more fearless and free
my hops will become.

To love oneself is the foundation of
love for other bunnies.

*No one can take bunniness
away from me.*

The bunny who commits to finding bunniness
has already begun to discover it.

Ϋ

In a field of clover, one must not
think of carrots. In a field of carrots,
one must not think of clover.

Ϋ

The wise bunny knows it does not
take effort to enjoy a fresh carrot.

Every hop we hop resonates throughout
the entire universe.

✕

I am a bunny, and I do bunny things.
It doesn't make me good, bad, right, or
wrong. It just makes me a bunny.

✕

The renunciation of doing harm is
the perfection of bunniness.

Working toward peace is not the same as
avoiding conflict with other bunnies.

Y

There is nothing wise about being
an unhappy bunny.

Y

As long as a bunny feels as though
he is the center of the universe, he will
not experience bunniness.

The wise bunny is tolerant with the intolerant and mild with the violent.

May I be true to my bunny nature even when faced with those who want me to be a fish or a bird.

One must be mindful of the bunniness and not the faults in others.

The wise bunny knows one can
always hop toward the light but must
never touch the flame.

It is neither the grass nor
the wind that moves. It is the bunny
mind that moves.

Y

Bunniness is the path and not
the destination; a hop with full
conviction is full victory.

Y

A bunny can't grow if he is always
trying to avoid suffering.

The only real failure in life is not
to be true to one's own bunny nature.

⋎

A foolish bunny who thinks himself
wise is foolish indeed.

⋎

When what one thinks and
where one hops are in harmony,
bunniness will follow.

A bunny who forgets to sit becomes
very tired of hopping.

꒦

A wise bunny pays no attention to
things done or left undone by others,
and considers only what he himself has
done or left undone.

꒦

The bunny who sees a problem
and does not help solve it does not
know bunniness.

May no bunny encounter me without
hopping away happier.

Wise and honorable hops flow naturally
from a heart that knows bunniness.

As a rock remains unshaken
by wind, the wise bunny remains
unshaken by blame and praise.

The gateway to bunniness is often
disguised as adversity.

I would rather hop and see
what happens than sit and worry about
what might go wrong.

A thoughtful bunny, together
with other thoughtful bunnies,
will put an end to pain.

❦

The wise bunny guards his thoughts, for,
unguarded, they hop all over the place.

❦

My responsibility is not only
to other bunnies, it is to all
creatures everywhere.

Bunniness can only be found when we stop struggling with what is beyond our control.

⋎

I know I feel like hopping,
but I do not have to hop.

⋎

The wise bunny thinks not of the carrot already munched, but rather of the carrots that remain to be munched.

Other bunnies may influence me, but I am
responsible for choosing my own hops.

$\vee$

In bunniness, a bunny can have
no shortcomings.

$\vee$

My frustration with other
bunnies shows me the parts of myself
I have yet to understand.

As the bee collects nectar without
harming the flower, so may bunnies live
in peace with one another.

One must find one's own way,
even if it means hopping where no bunny
has hopped before.

᭼

No bunny is really evil, though
they may be led astray.

᭼

The wise bunny knows that courage is
not the absence of fear but the willingness
to experience it directly.

Once you know bunniness,
hopping, sitting, or lying down,
everything you do is bunniness.

Ⅴ

One must munch a head of
cabbage leaf by leaf.

Ⅴ

The biggest delusion of bunnies
is the thought that I am here and
other bunnies are there.

Bunnies inflict pain on
others in the selfish pursuit of
their own satisfaction.

꙳

Sometimes bunniness means
taking the time to focus on another
bunny's troubles.

꙳

A bunny who hops with compassion lights
the way for all other bunnies.

Bunniness means being free from
hatred even among those who hate.

I am not this soft bunny body,
these long ears, or this fluffy cottontail.
I am my bunny nature.

The wise bunny knows that
the river cannot remain still and
the mountain cannot flow.

꙳

To hop safely through the maze
of life, one needs the light of wisdom and
the guidance of bunniness.

꙳

One must take the time
to distinguish between frivolous hops
and hops with purpose.

Bunniness does not come to one
who is too sure of his own ideas.

∀

Every hop can be hopped with love.

∀

A reckless bunny who becomes
sober brightens the world like the moon
when freed from clouds.

Sometimes a bunny must
hop through fear to find the
path to freedom.

᭶

The wise bunny knows even a
blade of grass is a wonder when he
really takes time to notice it.

᭶

Bunniness exists wherever there
is confidence in defenselessness.

One will not find peace while the thorn of hatred dwells in his bunny heart.

⋎

To be born into a field of clover and never munch the clover would be a grievous error.

⋎

Change exists. Resisting it, one suffers. Accepting it, one finds bunniness.

A bunny looking for carrots must
be careful not to overlook the cabbage.

May all bunnies think beautiful thoughts
and hop beautiful hops.

✲

A kind bunny must give up frowning
and grimacing, be the first to greet, and
be cuddly to all the world.

✲

The best way to find bunniness is to
lose oneself in helping others.

The wise bunny knows the fear of hopping
is often worse than the hop itself.

✦

There is no way to bunniness,
bunniness is the way.

✦

A bunny escaped from the
mouth of the wolf must not turn
back to be devoured.

The bunny who only does what he already does well will never reach higher goals.

Bunniness means choosing to love whatever gets in our way until it ceases to be an obstacle.

Only a strong bunny can hop the path of nonviolence.

That I stray from bunniness is
to be expected; more important is
that I return.

The wise bunny knows the tide will
rush out just as it rushes in.

Bunniness can only come after one
has seen the depths of sorrow.

꙳

Every bunny stumbles before
he learns to hop.

꙳

The wise bunny knows this
moment is more than just preparation
for something else.

If I focus on where bunniness went,
I will not be ready when it next arrives.

⁂

May we all hop in kindness,
for kind hops benefit all beings.

⁂

Pain will come. The wise bunny
accepts it with grace, knowing
it will also pass.

One must be kind, for every bunny
is fighting a hard battle.

The wise bunny knows carrots can
be stolen but bunniness cannot.

Noble bunnies neither praise
themselves nor disparage others.

To live peacefully with other
bunnies, one must first make peace
with oneself.

❦

All the miseries, evils, and
sufferings that arise from the world pass
away in the face of bunniness.

❦

A carrot buried in mud is just as
valuable as a carrot unearthed.

There is no such thing as a
ready-made path; a bunny must hop
to create her own.

The wise bunny knows life is not difficult
when one is open to all possibilities.

✲

When I hop into a bush of thorns,
I must remember there are bushes that
do not have thorns.

✲

The bunny body wears out
and grows old, but the virtue of
bunniness never will.

One must hop carefully, for every
hop has the potential to cause pain.

Just as a candle cannot burn without fire,
a bunny cannot live without bunniness.

It is not carrots but the
desire for more and more carrots
that leads bunnies astray.

The sun and moon shine alike
on those who practice bunniness and
those who do not.

✴

A bunny will sink if she does
not try to swim.

✴

A wise bunny sees more from inside
the den than a foolish bunny sees from
the mountaintop.

An awareness of light sustains a
bunny even when it is dark.

I am but a small part of bunniness,
just as a grain of salt is but a
small part of the sea.

Being around a destructive
bunny is itself destructive.

⁎

A wise bunny is wary of the
word "should" because it usually indicates
a preconceived judgment.

⁎

Bunniness comes to the bunny who
no longer delights in quarrels.

Breathing in, I know my long ears
are cold. Breathing out, I smile, knowing
I can experience cold.

☙

The wise bunny finds joy in giving,
and bunniness is his reward.

☙

I must remember much can
be learned from bunnies who
disagree with me.

By amending my mistakes,
I gain bunniness. By defending
my faults, I betray it.

❧

I can't always wait for someone
to tell me to hop.

❧

A wise bunny can leave any field
of clover because she knows the field
of clover does not define her.

The only barriers between
me and other bunnies are the
ones I put there.

❦

May no bunny suffer because of me.

❦

By choosing to stay when one can
no longer stand the present moment,
one moves closer to bunniness.

If a bunny who enjoys a lesser
carrot beholds a greater one, let him leave
aside the lesser to gain the greater.

The wise bunny knows not
to make major decisions from a
state of unbalance.

꒳

Great acts are made up of
many small hops.

꒳

No bunny can tell me the secret
to bunniness because no bunny knows
what it looks like to me.

The bunny who is truly himself is awake among sleeping bunnies.

⋎

One cannot develop bunniness by hopping away from adversity.

⋎

A bunny who refuses to face the dark will never see the stars.

The wise bunny knows that anger does nothing to protect one from harm.

✽

No kind hop ever stops with itself.

✽

We are all part of the universal bunniness; we are just at different places along the path.

When a bunny falls, he does not assign blame; he reawakens his original intention and hops again.

Bunniness neither begins nor ends with me.

A bunny must accept good and
evil alike, neither welcoming one nor
shrinking from the other.

⋎

Every failed hop is one hop
closer to success.

⋎

The wise bunny knows both
the sunshine and the rain help
the carrot grow.

When the bunny mind is pure, joy follows
like one's own fluffy cottontail.

❦

Love is not contingent upon another
bunny being lovable.

❦

Neither fire nor wind, birth
nor death can erase the bunniness
we extend to others.

Life is only ordinary to the
bunny who fails to recognize how
extraordinary it can be.

ༀ

My hops are my voice,
and they speak loudly.

ༀ

The wise bunny knows
bunniness is here, even if here is
not where she intended to be.

It is often the bunny we
least understand who needs our
compassion the most.

✧

Whatever it is, it is my path,
and I will continue hopping.

✧

Searching for bunniness means
not considering yourself an obstacle
to yourself.

The wise bunny is diligent today,
for tomorrow may be too late.

❦

To eat carrots I have never
eaten before, I must hop where I have
never hopped before.

❦

May we all dwell in the great
bunniness free from passion, aggression,
and prejudice.

Acknowledgments

Even as it began to come together, I couldn't believe that Bunny Buddhism was going to be a book. It never would have been a book at all without the support of Perigee Books and the encouragement of editor in chief extraordinaire, Marian Lizzi. I have to thank Marian in particular for believing in Bunny Buddhism from the beginning and for championing the idea of a book before the thought had even occurred to me. Special thanks also go to editorial assistant Lauren Becker for her assistance throughout the process. Additionally, I want to express my heartfelt gratitude to Durell Godfrey for her beautiful illustrations that truly capture the essence of Bunny Buddhism. Many thanks as well to the artists and illustrators who submitted artwork samples considered for this book. I would have been proud to work with any one of them, and I regret that it simply was not possible.

On a personal note, I want to thank my parents, Richard and Sandra Lester, who have exemplified patience and compassion by always loving me, even when I made it incredibly difficult. Many thanks to my husband, Rob Tebeau, for listening to me talk about Bunny Buddhism for years on end and for being there to support me as my meditation practice uncovered decades of repressed emotions that came out in messy bursts of tears and anger. Thanks to my siblings for sharing in my excitement about the book and for supporting my creative endeavors in general. Thanks to the world's greatest boss-turned-friend, Paul Kelley, for hearing me say I was interested in learning more about Buddhism and taking the next step of sharing with me some books by Pema Chödrön and Thich Nhat Hanh that completely changed my life. Thanks to each and every Buddhist writer who has influenced me over the years. Thanks to Profound Existence, the Boston Dharma Punx chapter, for welcoming me into their meditation group during a time of personal crisis. Thanks to Dennis Plant for helping me believe in myself. Thanks to the writing instructors who helped shape my life in sometimes painful ways. Thanks to my friends, colleagues, and coworkers, whose enthusiasm for Bunny Buddhism helped me believe it was a project worth continuing. Last, but certainly not least, I want to thank each and every person who has followed @BunnyBuddhism on Twitter, especially those whose positive comments made me believe there was a reason to continue spreading love and joy in a world that makes it so much easier to be negative.

Further Reading

Bayda, Ezra. *Being Zen: Bringing Meditation to Life*. Boston: Shambhala, 2003.

Bayda, Ezra. *Beyond Happiness: The Zen Way to True Contentment*. Boston: Shambhala, 2011.

Bodhi, Bhikkhu. *In the Buddha's Words: An Anthology of Discourses from the Pali Canon*. Somerville, MA: Wisdom Publications, 2005.

Brach, Tara. *Radical Acceptance: Embracing Your Life with the Heart of a Buddha*. New York: Bantam, 2004.

Chödrön, Pema. *Don't Bite the Hook: Finding Freedom from Anger, Resentment, and Other Destructive Emotions*. Boston: Shambhala, 2007.

Chödrön, Pema. *Getting Unstuck: Breaking Your Habitual Patterns and Encountering Naked Reality*. Louisville, CO: Sounds True, 2006.

Chödrön, Pema. *The Places That Scare You: A Guide to Fearlessness in Difficult Times*. Boston: Shambhala, 2002.

Chödrön, Pema. *When Things Fall Apart: Heart Advice for Difficult Times*. Boston: Shambhala, 2000.

His Holiness the Dalai Lama and Howard C. Cutler, MD. *The Art of Happiness: A Handbook for Living* (10th anniv. ed.). New York: Riverhead, 2009.

Goddard, Dwight. *A Buddhist Bible.* Boston: Beacon Press, 1994.

Hanh, Thich Nhat. *Anger: Wisdom for Cooling the Flames.* New York: Riverhead, 2002.

Hanh, Thich Nhat. *Awakening of the Heart: Essential Buddhist Sutras and Commentaries.* Berkeley, CA: Parallax Press, 2012.

Hanh, Thich Nhat. *Being Peace.* Berkeley, CA: Parallax Press, 2005.

Hanh, Thich Nhat. *You Are Here: Discovering the Magic of the Present Moment.* Boston: Shambhala, 2010.

Kabat-Zinn, Jon. *Guided Mindfulness Meditation (Series 1).* Louisville, CO: Sounds True, 2005.

Levine, Noah. *Against the Stream: A Buddhist Manual for Spiritual Revolutionaries.* New York: HarperOne, 2007.

Levine, Noah. *Dharma Punx.* New York: HarperOne, 2004.

Rinpoche, Yongey Mingyur. *Joyful Wisdom: Embracing Change and Finding Freedom.* New York: Harmony, 2010.

Rinpoche, Yongey Mingyur. *The Joy of Living: Unlocking the Secret and Science of Happiness.* New York: Harmony, 2008.

Suzuki, Shunryu. *Zen Mind, Beginner's Mind: Internal Talks on Zen Meditation and Practice.* Boston: Shambhala, 2011.

About the Author

Krista Lester is a writer, musician, and all-around creative spirit who discovered Buddhism in her early thirties and credits it with teaching her the meditation techniques she needed to manage a lifelong struggle with depression, anxiety, panic attacks, and chronic pain. She grew up near Pittsburgh, Pennsylvania, before moving to Boston, Massachusetts, to earn a bachelor of music in vocal performance from Boston University and a master of liberal arts in extension studies with a focus in literature and creative writing from Harvard University. She currently works as a music teacher and university administrator in the Greater Boston area, where she lives with her husband, Rob, and their dog, Salem.